COMBATIVE CONGRESS

Your Voice, Your Power

TOM MAST

Published by Solve American Gridlock LLC

ISBN: 979-8-9892354-0-7 (Paperback)
979-8-9892354-1-4 (eBook)

Dedication

I dedicate this book to my lovely wife, Eddie Mast. She has been very kind to tolerate the time I spent researching and writing on this important topic.

Contents

PART I — PROLOGUE

PART II — PREFACE

PART III — HISTORY

PART IV — ROOT CAUSES

PART V — MORE THAN TWO PARTIES

PART VI — OPEN PRIMARIES

PART VII — MULTI-MEMBER DISTRICTS

PART VIII — RANKED CHOICE VOTING

PART IX — CONCLUSION

PART I

PROLOGUE

Prologue

I have been very fortunate, and I owe society a lot for my happy and interesting times. I am genuinely concerned about the odds that my children, grandchildren, and everyone else have of enjoying similar opportunities. So, you have a retired mechanical engineer interested in working on important problems, not just their symptoms.

Like many Americans, my confidence in some of the major institutions important to our future has deteriorated over the decades, especially in the past few years, causing deep worry about our country. Congress is particularly troubled and needs to make several course changes. We can stimulate those changes; solutions are available, but first, we must understand them. Please remember that we are the supreme source of power! The vast majority of voters believe Congress is doing an inadequate job (graph below). What we must do, in conjunction with like-minded organizations and individuals, is to **insist** on the proper reforms.

The book contains several graphics to give the reader a good visual picture of important data and trends and to reinforce the text and photographs I have taken over the years. Many are upbeat and

A recipe for Congress is somewhat more complex than one for a church chili cookoff – but doable!

pleasant to provide balance and reinforcement to the serious messages about what we must do to improve our electoral systems for those following us.

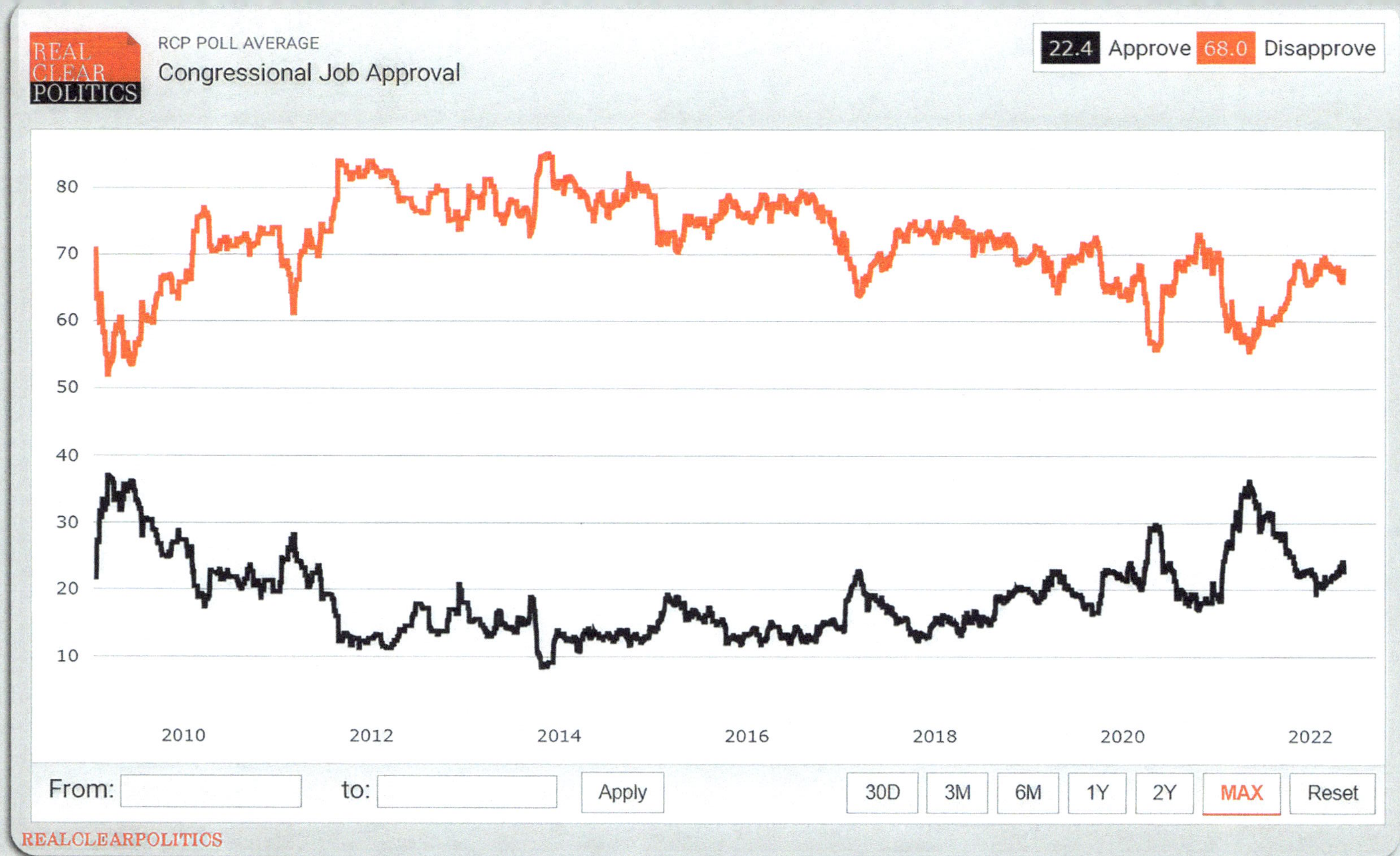
REAL CLEAR POLITICS
RCP POLL AVERAGE
Congressional Job Approval
22.4 Approve 68.0 Disapprove
80
70
60
50
40
30
20
10
2010
2012
2014
2016
2018
2020
2022
From:
to:
Apply
30D
3M
6M
1Y
2Y
MAX
Reset
REALCLEARPOLITICS

PART II

PREFACE

1

About this Book

The book is purposely short and a quick and pleasant read. It provides a good analysis of the dysfunction of our combative Congress, digs into the root causes, and proposes needed changes – all in sufficient and concise detail. It provides excellent references for additional research.

This **HANDBOOK** is all the reader needs to understand in a couple of hours our combative Congress. It is designed to alert Americans of every stripe to the dangers of the dysfunctions in our Congress, provide an understanding of their fundamental causes, demonstrate that they can be corrected, and indicate pathways to solutions. We recognize this is a daunting task, but other citizens and organizations are increasingly rising to the occasion.

The approach includes being logical, transparent, and nonpartisan. We ask, "Why? Why? Why?" digging down to the root causes of problems.

"...Benjamin Franklin, who, on leaving the Constitutional Convention of 1787, supposedly told a curious passerby that the Framers had produced ***a republic, if you can keep it.'"***

— *Adam J. White,* The Atlantic.

NY Harbor and the Statue of Liberty in a Beautiful Sunset – America!

National constitutions have lasted an average of only 17 years since 1789. Our republic's Constitution has lasted over 230 years! However, it is no secret that a huge percentage of the populace is increasingly worried that we have lost the ability and fortitude to formulate and implement solutions to serious problems. A symptom of this is gridlock, but attacking symptoms is futile; one must dig down to the root causes.

Dysfunctional Congress: There are reasons why our electoral systems have fallen behind those of other major democracies; we will see later in the book that our two parties created these systems to reduce competition. Key changes are needed; the understanding and push for reforms should come from US Citizens.

Gridlock: According to Merriam-Webster, gridlock refers to a situation in which both sides of a conflict reach a stalemate or impasse, with neither party able to achieve victory or willing to yield. It can also be described as a deadlock, halt, logjam, Mexican standoff, or standstill. These terms convey the same idea of a deadlock or impasse.

Objective: Our objective is to analyze the root causes for the dysfunction of Congress, encourage a broad understanding of them, and describe corrective reforms.

We have drifted over the past few decades, especially lately, into a situation where our bipolar—the Republican Party and the Democratic Party—political system seems to think the highest calling is to harm the opposing party. Very few advanced democracies have painted themselves into this corner of having only two effective parties; their legislators must and can use negotiation to solve problems.

We, citizens, must take the reins and work on our governmental gridlock and all its causes. There are solutions!

In 2014, about 95% of incumbent congressional candidates were returned to office, but the approval rate for Congress was around 14%. ***How in the world can that be?*** The simple answer is that we have broken electoral systems.

2

Excerpts from a Letter to Congress

"***Houston, we have a problem,***" someone at NASA commented about one of the Apollo 13 manned missions.

Congress has shown itself to be increasingly polarized and ineffective in addressing its tasks; this applies to both parties. Ballotpedia polled the congressional approval rating at 17% on February 18, 2022. It is not a stretch to say that most members of Congress are aware of the problem and increasingly dissatisfied with the present electoral methods and their personal status.

Revising electoral methods that nourish the evolution of more than two parties will stimulate more points of view and negotiation, as has been demonstrated in virtually all developed nations. This greater diversity creates a climate for solving problems. Our two parties devote too much of their attention to battles rather than problem-solving.

America has always had a "can-do" spirit.

It is needed now more than ever!

3

Conversation with Bill

My son, Bill, called me from Michigan. He was quite concerned about several aspects of Biden's recent announcement of his intention to cancel considerable student debt, $300 billion this year, according to the WSJ, whose source was the Penn Wharton Budget Model. Setting aside the politics of the matter, Bill said he was having trouble knowing how this could be done because he had the understanding that no act of Congress had authorized this loan forgiveness. In fact, Speaker Pelosi publicly said that Congress would have to pass a law to cancel this student debt.

Let's focus our attention on how Bill, a company president, valedictorian, and holder of three college degrees, could be wondering what is going on. If he is confused about how our government does things, millions of other citizens must be in the same boat, and the media don't help matters.

The President has said he plans to use an Executive Order to forgive student loans. A quick Internet search reveals that executive orders have been used for a long time. However, it does seem that recent presidents of both parties had the attitude that if Congress doesn't pass what they want, they will get it some other way, like signing an Executive Order—an approach that the Founding Fathers of our country did not have in mind when they strove to balance the powers of the three branches. It also seems that Executive Orders have been extended to more expensive and important matters. Congress has the power to prevent a president from forgiving debt owed to our government, in this instance, several hundred billion dollars.

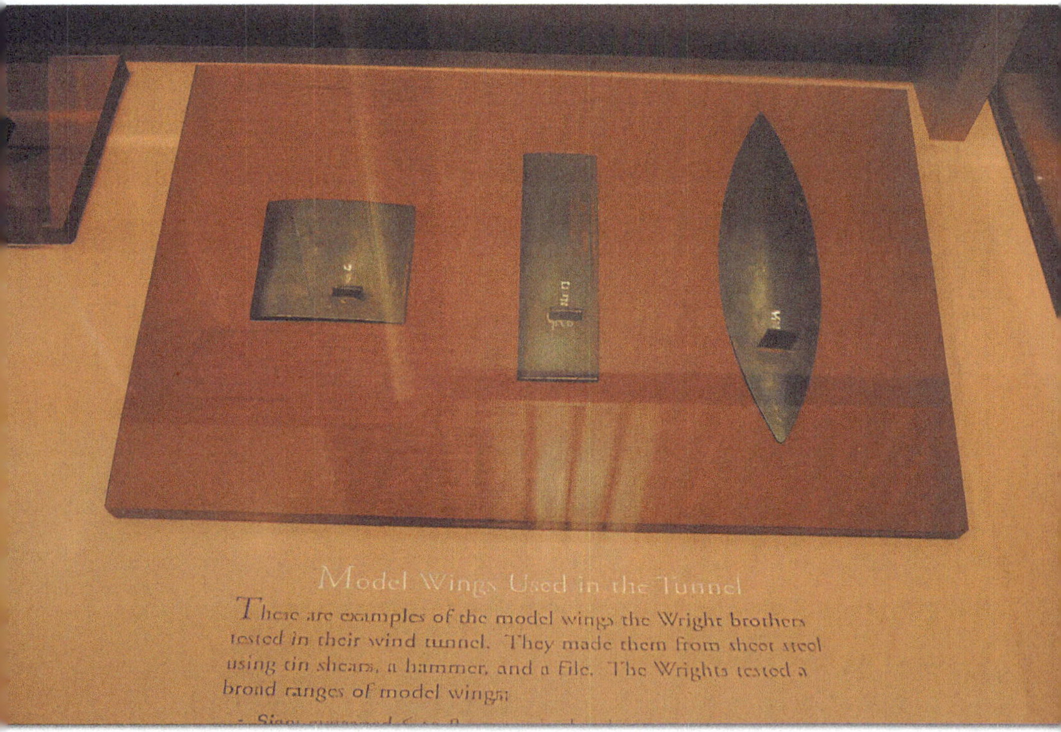

We Americans are problem solvers! This example from a Smithsonian exhibit shows how the Wright Brothers approached the problem of determining the lift and drag of wings. They designed a machine to test various airfoils.

This sad situation is another symptom of Congress' lack of problem-solving capabilities. We probably can agree that it is overloaded with responsibilities. But its dysfunction caused by the perpetual combat between two parties, almost evenly divided in size and numbers, has led to a general perception that it can't get the job done. Now, this doesn't mean that just because it will not pass a certain piece of legislation, it is dysfunctional; after all, bad ideas arise in Congress and deserve to fail. However, Congress has been leaving huge issues (see partial list in the "Surgery for Congress" chapter) lying on the table unsolved, and it has an approval rating among the public that has been hovering around 20% for some time, lower than virtually all other classes of organizations. The issue at hand had consistently deteriorated over time, spanning different periods when both parties had control of Congress.

The problem extends to international matters. Congress even voluntarily and formally gave up some of its powers under the Constitution to declare war, with the result that we haven't had good advice and counsel and statutory checks on presidential war-making powers for a long time.

Congress has relinquished some of its powers to the Executive and Judicial Branches. This is unfortunate since the Legislative Branch is closest to the people because its members are elected.

So, we have a problem. What do we do about it? We, citizens, need to be problem solvers like the Wright Brothers! Congress must reclaim some of its prestige and powers to balance our federal government better. What are the root causes and solutions for our combative Congress?

This book's mission is to answer that question!

4

Congressional Elections – Do They Work Well?

We had an election for Congress in November 2022. Unfortunately, it was unsurprising to learn that our two parties were elected with very narrow margins in each chamber. ***Again!***

We have two all-powerful political parties, contrasting with most other respected world democracies. One outcome of this election was that each chamber of Congress was still controlled by one or the other party, meaning the Democratic Party or Republican Party. Since both parties are so similar in size, the power will be almost evenly divided in each chamber. Because of the nature of two opposing entities for power – much like that of two children – their relationship has degenerated into a constant encounter. A change in power in one of the chambers in these times immediately results in the newly empowered party beginning to unwind what the other party just finished. The parties tend to vote in blocks because winning is more important to them than solving the country's problems. The ultimate result of the election will be "more of the same" in that the fighting will continue, but perhaps with somewhat of a shift of power, the *see-saw effect*.

How did we end up in such a predicament? How did we corner ourselves? The answer isn't trivial but is vital to the future of our country. So, we must ask ourselves what is wrong.

We are too sleepy to realize what is happening.

Why has polarization and division in Congress accelerated so much in recent years? It is a complex issue that has troubled many of us. Congress has undergone a pronounced division into two blatantly opposing factions. As explored carefully in this book, the division we observe predominantly originates from an unwavering thirst for control and a relentless pursuit of employing increasingly powerful strategies.

This affects the media and the public, and in turn, they affect what happens in Congress. Positions harden. The far left and the far right have become more aggressive and combative. Parties have become firmer in ostracizing unruly members, making it risky and unpleasant for them to deviate. It is unfortunate and dysfunctional for members of Congress not to feel free to vote their conscience. Any reduction of polarization in Congress, the media, or the public will likely create improvements in the other two.

There is a growing recognition that our current election system is problematic and rigged. It is designed in such a way to favor the two major political parties, the Republicans and Democrats, allowing them to maintain their authority and influence over their constituents and other political parties. This strategy creates a duopoly, where these two parties control the political landscape. As a result, it becomes exceedingly difficult for candidates from any other political party to secure election victories.

In certain aspects of our electoral system, the first-past-the-post method is still employed, allowing a candidate to secure victory in an election with a plurality, not a majority. This can produce results not proportional to those voting.

The two leading parties in America stood to gain by not having competition from other parties. How did we sleep through the process of our current electoral methods being put firmly in place by the two strong parties—the Democratic Party and Republican Party—over the past few decades? My son, Steve, suggested a metaphor. The electoral methods were like invasive plants, kudzu in the south and juniper in Texas and Mexico, that choke out competitive plants.

Electoral methods are important – vitally important! They are a little complex and represent change that makes voters somewhat hesitant. However, most of these rules are used internationally and increasingly by state and local governments. Congress and state legislatures, run by our two parties, created the methods now in use. We, the people, can insist on changes, and we should do so before it is too late.

> ***"The definition of insanity is doing the same thing over and over again and expecting a different result."***
>
> ***—Albert Einstein.***

5

Safe Seats

The term "safe seat" refers to a political situation where a particular party or incumbent has high security. According to Wikipedia, a safe seat is fully secure for either a specific party, an incumbent, or both. On the other hand, FiveThirtyEight defines a safe seat as one with at least a 5% advantage in elections.

We are well aware of gerrymandering in the United States contributing to the significant number of secure seats in the House of Representatives. According to the definition provided by Merriam-Webster, gerrymandering refers to the manipulation of electoral districts to provide an unfair advantage to one political party. Dave Wasserman, an analyst at the nonpartisan Cook Political Report, estimated in February 2022 that approximately 94% of representatives will compete in districts considered safe for their party. This statistic highlights how gerrymandering has intensified the lack of competitive races in the House.

The general election winner of a safe seat will almost always be determined by the party holding that seat at the time of the election. This means that the important discourse in campaigns is intraparty, taking place within the closed primaries of the two parties. And with safe seats, we almost always know which of those parties will win in the general election. This further means that there is reduced campaigning between the two parties, fewer points of view being aired, and more adoption of the party line in the safe districts, giving voters only one choice. No wonder we have polarization! No wonder voter turnout is so poor!

Our two-party system is a cause for polarization, which is a cause for congressional dysfunction. Safe seats tend to lock us into having only two parties. Gerrymandering enables the creation of safe seats by the party in power in each state at the time of the census every decade. Single-member districts are the foremost cause of safe seats. See also the chapter Analyzing Congress's single-member District Mandate.

6

Proportional Voting

"Proportional voting" means that the results of an election are as proportional to the desires of the voters in that election as practicable.

According to the ACE Electoral Knowledge Network, some form of proportional representation is used for national lower-house elections in approximately 94 countries. Ranked Choice Voting (RCV) methodology significantly improves proportionality.

Voters get to rank from a choice of several candidates. Before the second round, the candidate with the least number of votes is eliminated, and the second-place votes from that candidate's poll are transferred to the remaining candidates.

This repeats as necessary until a candidate has a majority. It is called Instant Runoff Voting because this process ***is*** the runoff, avoiding the time, expense, and poor voter turnout of a traditional runoff.

Since voters get to express a preference for more than one candidate, the final winner will be more proportional to those voting than in a first-past-the-post or winner-takes-all election or a runoff. The problem of having a very poor turnout for a runoff election disappears. RCV is rapidly catching on; Maine and Alaska have chosen to use it across the board, and other states and political entities use it for an increasing portion of their elections. There are other advantages including that it works to increase the number of effective parties beyond two. You can quickly learn more by pointing your browsers to the following websites:

www.fairvote.org
www.rcvfortexas.org
www.solveamericangridlock.com

We need to have more than two effective parties (meaning large enough to have some influence over policy) to make voting more proportional to the voters and to reduce the bipolar and see-saw nature of our present two-party system.

One can see from the following chart what an exception our United States Congress is by being "locked into" two parties.

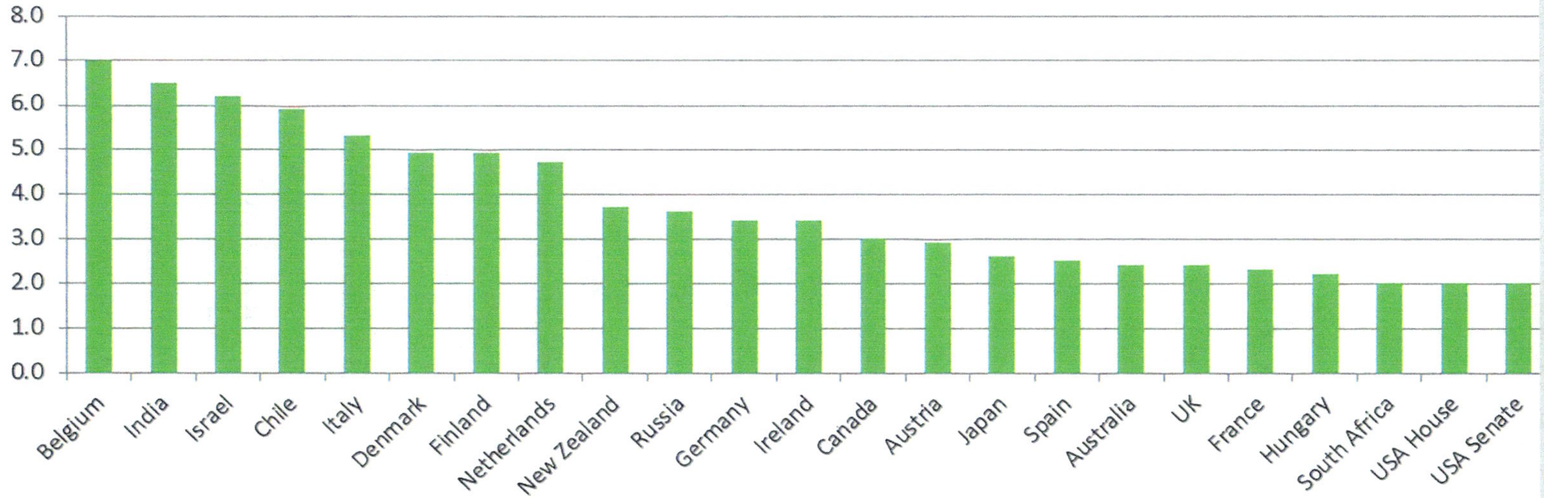

Effective number of Parties, non-USA Average 3.9

Data from The Politics of Electoral Systems

by Michael Gallagher and Paul Mitchell, 2005

7

Surgery for Congress

Problem

The United States Congress is facing a chronic and progressively worsening "electoral systems" disease that is intensifying numerous significant political, ethical, and social issues. Despite various ineffective interventions attempted in the past, the disease's symptoms continue to escalate, manifesting as a series of failures in almost every major sector within American culture and society. The severity and complexity of the situation necessitate an urgent and profound intervention, potentially of a surgical nature, to halt and reverse the progression of this debilitating disease. Here are a few <u>problems</u>:

- Congress has a chronic electoral system disease, degrading every passing year.
- Various ineffective interventions have been tried.
- This political and ethical disease has caused a long list of symptoms resulting in great anguish to people dependent on the patient. The <u>symptoms</u> include:

- o Failure to solve the US immigration issues.
- o Failure to stop the drug-related crisis.
- o Failure to tackle guns-related violence.
- o Failure in fiscal matters including budgeting, deficit spending, and a high percentage of overall spending on autopilot.
- o Failure to provide for the fiscal viability of major programs, including Social Security and Medicare.
- o Failure to stem the flow of congressional powers to the Executive and Judicial Branches.
- o Failure to develop a professional, comprehensive, and long-term plan for mitigating greenhouse gas emissions—the largest project America and the world have ever faced.
- o Failure to use regular order and procedures that worked well in the past.
- o Failure to allow fair competition from more than two parties.

The diagnosis of this dangerous condition is chronic "***electoral systems***" disease. It is time for surgical intervention.

OBJECTIVE

Metaphorically speaking, the objective is to surgically correct the electoral systems that have caused pain and obvious symptoms. This will lead to a recovery in congressional legislative procedures, resulting in a Congress whose existence and focus is on solving problems for the country and its people rather than interparty combat.

Nimitz Pacific War Museum
Our father and three uncles were doctors in WWII; two were surgeons.
Fifty family members honored them at Nimitz Museum.

THE SURGERY

Clear the obstructions to have useful interparty competition in Congress.

PART III
HISTORY

8

History

This home in New York state depicts our long and proud history.

Congressional Functionality Goes Downhill

Tale of Two Parties – History

Lee Drutman writes in **Breaking the Two-Party Doom Loop** about the views of **Madison, Washington, and John Adams** regarding political parties.

Madison said, "*Different leaders ambitiously contending for pre-eminence and power… have, in turn, divided mankind into parties, inflamed them with mutual animosity.*" The crisis comes when the state is "violently heated and distracted by the rage of party."

In his famous farewell address, Washington warned America about "*the alternate domination of one faction over another, sharpened by the spirit of revenge, natural to party dissension, which in different ages and countries has perpetrated the most horrid enormities.*"

President Adams spoke, "*A division of the republic into two great parties…is to be dreaded as the great political evil.*"

Incredible that these three great men were so farsighted! They articulated our woes of today two-and-a-third centuries ago.

"Political parties are the lifeline of a democratic governance … America's system was, therefore, designed to operate in an environment where most factions would be short-lived, developing over issues and then dissolving when those issues faded or were somehow resolved."

Adapted from The Role of Political Parties in Preventing Congress from Functioning, Dennis R. Bullock, Real Clear Policy.

To promote the alliance of different factions coming together temporarily to address various issues, we need a system that involves more than two parties. Such a system encourages the collaboration of diverse groups, allowing them to join forces and tackle problems collectively. By facilitating the formation of temporary alliances, this approach ensures that a wide range of perspectives and expertise are brought to the table. It fosters an environment where different factions can work together effectively, pooling their resources and efforts toward finding solutions. Ultimately, this inclusive and cooperative system enables the resolution of multiple challenges through temporary collaborations.

Political parties have existed in America almost since its inception. They are vital to the operation of a democratic government and are about the art and science of governing. Politics is fundamentally a way to sort out differences of opinion, so there will be disagreements – about policy, at least. However, there are choices about which **electoral systems** are used to select and organize governments, and they can influence how well the system works.

Two influential parties have existed for the most part since our country was formed. Until roughly the latter part of the twentieth century, the two-party system worked better than in the past two or three decades. Why was that?

For one thing, members of Congress used to socialize more, developing relationships with each other, including those of the other party. The advances in aviation and communications have made it easier for them to spend more time at home – spending less social time together in Washington. Regular order including the reliance on committees to lead members to work with one another well has almost disappeared as senior leaders choose issues and craft the legislation, often behind closed doors.

For most of the second half of the twentieth century, our country effectively had four parties. Two branches of the Democrats and the Republicans existed because each party had a conservative-leaning and a liberal-leaning wing. These four groups with various viewpoints had to cooperate to enact legislation; they required and enabled the necessary different perspectives, negotiations, and civility to govern. Congress functioned, passing considerable primary legislation with actual bipartisan voting. So, while America didn't have four parties, this situation proved the concept of needing more than two parties.

Around the mid-1990s, this semi-four-party situation began accelerating into a more rigid two-party position as some members left and new ones were elected. As the two main parties hardened in their views and became more combative, the civility assisted by the societal issues mentioned above faded, and the two parties implemented several electoral methods at both the state and federal levels that became significant hurdles for other parties to compete; stay tuned for details on these later in the book.

Leaders in Congress amassed much more power for themselves, leaving the other members with less meaningful roles. Bills have increasingly been created by the elite and put before the membership hurriedly and non-transparently, further aggravating most members. Politics in Congress was becoming a zero-sum game where every win for one party was a loss for the other. Bipartisan legislation of significance was almost a thing of the past. By around 2010, the two parties had stiffened their stances to basically being against whatever the other party wanted. The wild swings in ideological philosophy and legislative focus each time one party displaced the other in power stimulated efforts for the incoming party to undo what the previous party had done. These changes in direction irritated the citizens. Doesn't all this sound very familiar?

Our Founding Fathers had anticipated many issues, protecting against their maturing to severe problems with checks and balances among the three branches of government. But they did not include anything explicitly dealing with the present two-party standoff within the legislative branch in the Constitution. Our current two-party system fosters two opposed points of view—the Mexican standoff!

America is very much the exception in having effectively only two parties, meaning parties large enough to influence votes and policy. See the graph in the Proportional Voting chapter. Drutman says that in multiparty democracies, coalitions work and that America's two-party and "first-past-the-post" or single-winner plurality voting system is the global outlier.

What has been happening in Congress for the past decade? Regular order has all but disappeared! Per Wikipedia: Regular order within the context of the United States Congress refers to the semi-strict or strict application of committee and subcommittee processes, including public hearing opportunities and the holding of multiple votes. Said processes are designed to promote consensus-based decision-making, particularly in fostering accommodations for minority viewpoints.

Many members feel demeaned by the present ways of doing business, which often leads them to give up and prioritize the acquisition of prestige, money, and perks. This, in turn, allows a select few to effectively run Congress and exert control over the agenda as well as spending. The consequences of this dynamic are far-reaching and include a diminished level of respect for the Constitution, the rule of law, decorum, and interpersonal relationships. It's truly perplexing and disheartening to witness such outcomes.

The federal government tasks, including those of Congress, might have grown to an unmanageable size. However, even if we concede the veracity of this statement, it does not represent the root cause. A dysfunctional Congress does not serve as the fundamental cause but rather manifests as a symptom. The blame lies with our electoral systems, which obstruct the attainment of a Congress that operates seamlessly.

www.fairvote.org
www.rcvfortexas.org
www.solveamericangridlock.com

PART IV
ROOT CAUSES

9

The Root Cause of a Problem

Problem

Congress is not doing its job well. Of course, we would like Congress to do an outstanding job, tackling and solving our significant issues – and others, too – on a timely basis and in ways satisfactory to most voters. In any effort to make corrections, we must guard diligently against the common temptation to work on symptoms rather than root causes. This isn't an easy task. Fortunately, many level heads in this country have addressed themselves to this effort. One must drill down to find root causes.

A Japanese Quality Control Technique: Why? Why? Why?

The Japanese "Why? Why?" Technique, widely recognized in manufacturing and engineering circles, is valuable for uncovering the underlying cause(s) of quality or reliability issues. Its effectiveness is evident in Japan's remarkable achievement of capturing approximately half of the U.S. automobile market in the late 1900s, primarily attributed to its superior quality and reliability. Let's delve into an illustrative example of the Why? Why? Why? Technique: the failure of an automobile alternator bracket.

Why did the automobile alternator bracket fail? Because the steel used was weak. Why was the steel weak? Because the factory employed multiple grades of steel to produce the brackets. Why were various grades of steel used? Multiple grades of steel were used because the procurement specifications were inadequately written and lacked clarity. Why were the specifications poorly written? Because a recently hired engineer was responsible for drafting them. Why was the engineer unable to produce satisfactory specifications? Because he received insufficient training and supervision.

It is truly astonishing that, without meticulous exploration, the root cause of a bracket failure might not have been traced back to a deficiency in the engineering department's supervision.

The effort to identify the root causes of Congress's Dysfunctionality will be evident in this book. Such root causes make solutions much more visible.

My grandfather clock was created about the same time as our nation. Tender loving care and good maintenance have it keeping time within an average of one minute per week.

Congress deserves the same attention.

10

Block Voting

Congress has plunged headlong into a state of near-complete party-driven voting, with nearly 100% adherence to block voting. The extent of this phenomenon should leave everyone bewildered. Why has this happened? What underlying factors compel numerous members of Congress to cast their votes contrary to their personal convictions and the desires of their constituents?

Reasons include careerism, led by the need for support and money in the next election; fear of the power of congressional leaders to disrupt careers; power and prestige of being on the winning team and a desire for my team to win the next election; having only two influential parties that reduce most topics to polarization or winner-take-all arguments; getting caught up in the game of crushing the other party; the enormous volume and variety of federal commitments: safe seats; first-past-the-post voting methods. The reasons in this list are symptoms. We must dig deeper to isolate the root causes.

Do some members of Congress buck the system and not cooperate with their party leaders? One can think of examples, and they are often to be admired for doing what they feel is right. However, the wrath of the party can and does destroy their careers rather than listening to their suggestions. This is very sad. What can we do? Create electoral systems fostering more than two parties.

The sun has set on many countries, including the Soviet Union.
Don't let it happen here!

11

Careerism

Single-member districts enable and foster careerism. Dictionary entries and even Wikipedia offer negative interpretations of careerism, but let's cut to the chase: it's an unwavering obsession with preserving one's position, often disregarding the commitment to excel. What ignites this puzzling phenomenon? The driving forces are power, prestige, perks, and money. These intoxicating incentives create a whirlwind of ambition, causing individuals to prioritize personal gain over genuine dedication to their responsibilities. It's a peculiar dance where the allure of influence and status entices individuals to forsake their true potential, leaving us baffled by the distortion of priorities within professional endeavors.

What are the Effects of Careerism?

- Careerism causes a shift of the members' focus from legislation and problem-solving to campaigning for reelection – including raising money.

Cooperating to solve problems works so well.

- It effectively disenfranchises many voters, giving them a representative or senator who doesn't care enough or work diligently to respond to voters' problems.
- This results in voter apathy and poor election turnout, exacerbated if a district is a House single-member and safe one.
- It causes members to avoid risks when voting.
- The members may be more likely to pay attention to lobbyists than individual citizens.

- It causes intense allegiance to one's party, its successes, and its chances of winning – at the expense of solving America's problems.
- This focus on winning creates friction and competition with members of the other party, reducing negotiation to solve problems together. i.e., the *"Us. Vs. Them"* mentality.
- Careerism, coupled with power having gravitated to the elite leaders in Congress, can lead to boredom and money becoming more important to members than accomplishments.
- It leads to voters' feeling that they have no power to influence course corrections and thus leads to apathy and not voting.

In summary, careerism means a strong focus on getting reelected continually. Since House members stand for election every two years, they are often actively running for office – a huge distraction.

Extreme careerism is a symptom, not a root cause. It follows from the desire for power and prestige. This power makes a member more likely to get elected while reducing the pressure to solve problems for voters. We will see later that the root causes of a combative and dysfunctional Congress are mechanisms that allow excessive careerism.

Multi-member districts would correct most of the ills of single-member districts and are a tool against careerism. They also promote a more-than-two-party system, a very positive change.

12

Root Causes of the Student Loan Debt Crisis

Rachel Larimore, the managing editor of The Dispatch Weekly, penned an article on Very Expensive Week dated August 27, 2022. Her focus was the pressing problem of student loan debt.

Early in the article, she mentioned that the student debt forgiveness cost could approach $1 trillion and said that "…is that it's just one more sign that our political process is so broken that we are unable, or unwilling, to solve problems anymore." I agree. Let's find out why it is broken and how it can be fixed!

With some help from the executive branch, Congress created student loans and related programs that encouraged students to take risks involving degree selections and heavy debt they could not repay. These programs also created strong demand for higher education that stimulated the growth rate of tuition at 8%, about double that of inflation, and pricing many people entirely out of a college education over a few decades.

Congress was aware of these issues it nurtured but did not correct them. Now, the President has threatened to forgive some student debt by executive order, and the Speaker of the House has retorted

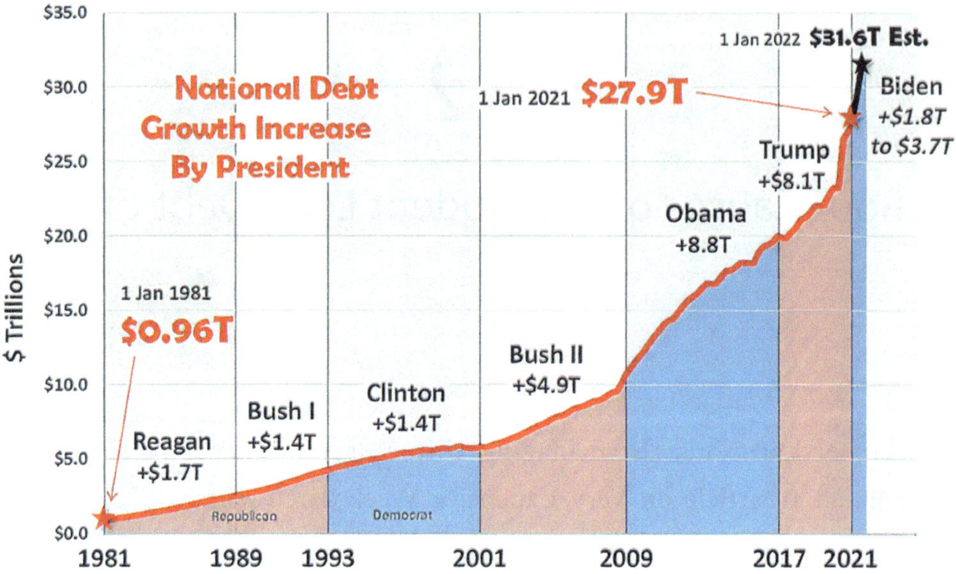

$30 trillion debt, 84 million families.
Therefore, $360,000 Gross U.S. Federal Debt per family.
(*Source:* www.jobenomics.com)

that only Congress can take such an action. Of course, the question remains whether Congress could agree on what to do and take some action. Almost all the time, there are only two points of view in our combative Congress, and with the typical tight balance between the powers of our two strong parties, gridlock ensues.

Rachel Larimore finished with, *"Just as there are no easy solutions to the big issues I've mentioned, there is no easy fix for our politics. We need to elect officials who are knowledgeable and qualified, and serious about problem-solving. But too many voters are drawn to candidates who, at best, have unserious ideas and, at worst, are just there to posture and dominate the other side. We can blame our elected officials for what they do or don't do, but we're the ones who put them there."*

We can fix the problem of having a dysfunctional Congress.

Root Cause Analysis

Why is our Congress dysfunctional?

Because taking rigid and often extreme positions has become the *modus operandi* of the two parties, often taking precedence over problem-solving.

Why have the two parties become more combative and less productive?

Because with the current election methods limiting Congress to two parties, inflicting pain on the other party is perceived as a better way to stay in power than solving the country's problems.

Why can the two parties restrict power to the two of them?

You won't believe it, but electoral systems used at both federal and state levels have been designed in a way that's like saying "no entry" to competition. Can you imagine that? It's like they don't want any challengers! It's ridiculous. They make it so only a few people have a shot at winning. So much for fairness!

What are the root causes of this exclusion of competition?

It's really mind-boggling when you think about it. These electoral systems we have in place favor our two main parties and shut out other parties. Can you believe it? It's like they're causing the problem themselves!

It's just so unfair and not very American!

So, the root causes of our student loan debt problem and many others are our electoral methods. The ones we use frequently produce results not proportional to the voting public and were ***designed*** to foster having only two viable parties whose primary goal is not problem-solving but domination over the other party. Electoral methods leading quickly to more than two influential parties are primaries open to multiple parties, multi-member districts, and ranked-choice voting (RCV). These electoral methods produce much more proportional voting meaning that the winners of elections closely represent the viewpoints and desires of the voters.

What, me worry? We, citizens, must drive reforms.

13

Animosity and Discord

It is only to be expected that competition will exist among intelligent and ambitious people. But, when relationships deteriorate to the point that they can be characterized by animosity and discord, damage is being done to the organization – Congress. Few would disagree that differences in recent years have led to unusually bitter and dysfunctional feelings among members. This is occurring both between and within the two political parties. Why?

Individual members are disillusioned that they don't have the power and influence they expected in their roles. Why is this? The striving for power between the two parties has led to a shifting of influence from members to party leaders, reduced responsibility, and authority of committees, downgrading of regular order including floor debate and open voting, and a lack of respect for individual opinions. Why did this happen? The emphasis on a party's winning legislative votes and elections has led to an unfortunate and dysfunctional centralization of power in Congress. Also, there is a feeling that the party in power can do anything it wants, leading to it taking inflexible positions to the left or right of the center.

Other conditions fuel polarization and ill feelings. Members are overloaded with the vast volume and variety of matters being handled by the federal government; there is no way a member can be competent in even a tiny fraction of these topics. Why? National issues grow naturally with population and as new topics are added – like the Internet, aviation, nuclear energy, and China trade. In addition, it also increases as the federal government takes on tasks formerly the responsibility of state and local governments. Rather than "Whose problem is this?" we now hear, "How and when is the federal government going to do something about this?"

Polarization in Congress is a huge problem, but it is baked into the cake. It is the product of our electoral systems. Our system of having only two parties is very much the exception for important nations, making a case that our zero-sum/winner-takes-all two-party system is a big reason for our difficulties. Of course, extreme friction in Congress spills over into the media and the public.

Members of Congress are overloaded but not allowed to exercise the powers they rightly believed they would have in Congress, creating apathy among many of them. Their hands are tied. The focus often is on checkmating the other party rather than solving our country's problems, resulting in our combative Congress. The two-party system we have in America is an essential reason for animosity and discord. What are the root causes of this system? Stay tuned; we will learn more in the following chapters.

14

Congress's Electoral Methods

This analysis and findings flow from the excellent book *The Politics Industry* by Katherine Gehl and Michael Porter, published in 2020. Ms. Gehl is a former business owner and executive who turned her efforts some years ago to political innovation. Mr. Porter is a professor at Harvard Business School and a famous author of over twenty management-related books. Together, they have carefully analyzed the fundamental issues with Congress and laid out badly needed reforms.

The authors see the problem as Congress's duopoly, which aims to "protect and perpetuate the politics industry itself and grow its power, not to produce results." They say the ***root cause*** is the political system, not certain parties, policies, or people. The two authors aim to create more "choice" – more competition. They want to stimulate action among us citizens, not merely analysis – although analysis is always necessary to ensure one is working on the real problem and coming up with the correct answers.

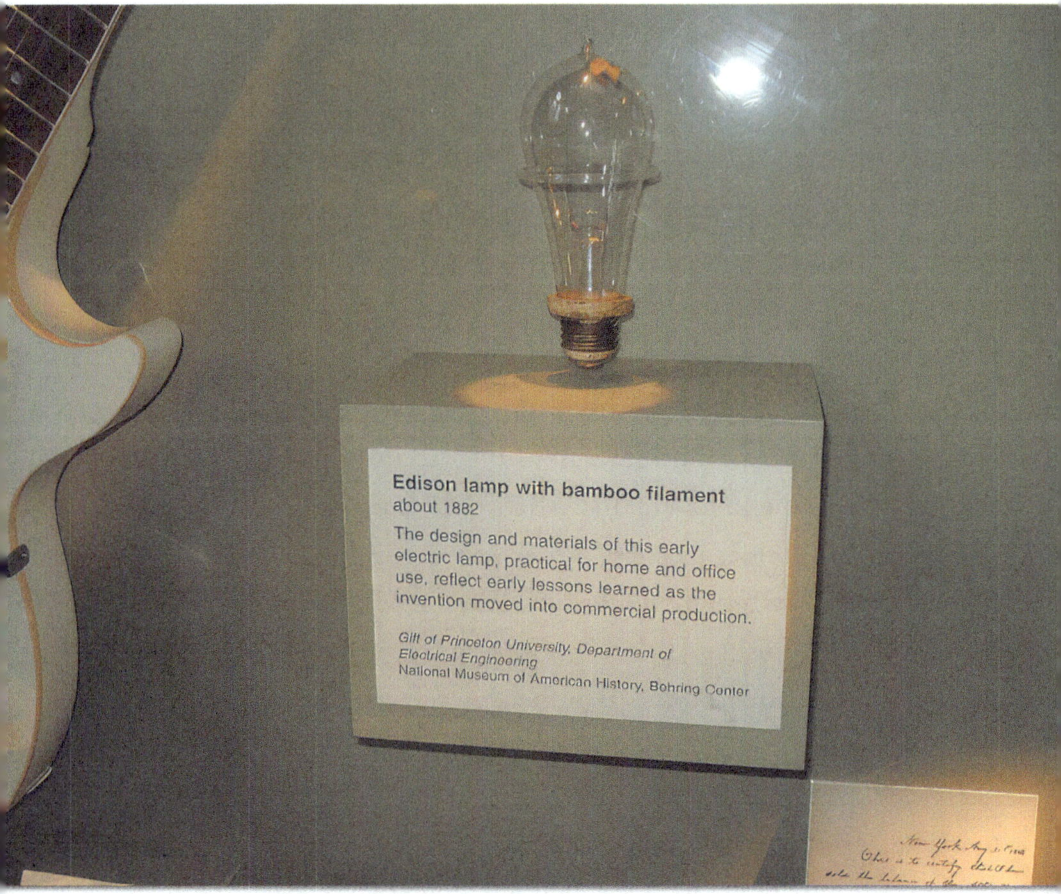

Americans have long tackled challenging problems aggressively – and solved them! Smithsonian Museum.

Their book emphasizes the importance of competition, not surprisingly, since Michael Porter has a teaching, writing, and consulting career in America's competitive business industries. One might say that we observe severe competition between America's only two significant political parties. Yes, they are combative, but it is primarily a competition for power, not problem-solving. The Congress duopoly colludes in designing and perpetuating the rules for elections. We have antitrust laws to prevent practices that stifle competition in business, but alas, the Politics Industry has no such brakes on its traditions. Most countries have avoided having this duopoly.

Gehl and Porter argue that the ***election machinery*** is a huge cause of our lack of competition in government. The two parties have successfully restricted new and small parties from participating fairly. The party primaries, cited in the book as the "eye of the needle," have evolved through efforts of the two parties at the state level to send a candidate from each of the major parties to the general election. These party primaries decide the winners, exacerbated by a federal statute and rules that have led to 80-90% of House seats being safe seats. These party primaries generally are poorly attended. In many states, candidates can win with less than a majority vote. It is complicated and intentionally very expensive for a new party to obtain the right to participate. If a third-party candidate with a fresh perspective does enter the competition, they are usually viewed as a "spoiler," one who is more likely to draw votes from one of the leading candidates than the other and thereby assist the voter's least favorite candidate toward a win. The result of the general election is that we often find ourselves holding our noses and voting for the lesser of two evils.

The lesser of two evils is still evil.

The US Constitution is very brief on election machinery for Congress. It says that the state legislatures have this job, then that "Congress may at any time by law make or alter such Regulations..." The state legislatures are populated *overwhelmingly* by the same two major parties.

The book quotes President John Adams, "There is nothing I dread so much as the division of the republic into two great parties, each arranged under its leader, and concerting measures in opposition to the other."

Gehl and Porter propose New Rules for election machinery. Final-Five voting would have open, single-ballot, nonpartisan primaries in which the top-five candidates qualify for the general election (called top-five primaries) and use ranked-choice voting (RCV) in general elections." These changes have been long overdue and carry immense significance! Picture this: with multi-member districts, several candidates would be selected to advance to the general election, more than the number of seats in that district. Ranked Choice Voting would be used to select proportional winners for the number of seats in that district.

The other topic is ***legislative machinery***, Congress's processes to create laws. The book says that the elections and legislative machinery are interdependent and that fixing both is much more powerful than selecting only one. However, it makes the point that the election's machinery changes must come first – which is correct. This book will only touch lightly here on "legislative machinery." It seems clear that fixing our electoral methods (election machinery) will lead to more competition and electing senators and representatives more focused on problem-solving than reelection. This will lead to repairs of the legislative machinery.

Many vital examples are cited in the book of the abuses of legislative processes. Budgeting is late, poorly done, and often ignored. Brinksmanship in budgeting, approval of debt ceilings, and essential bills is now standard. All too often, many issues are rolled into a giant piece of legislation, including some that would never have passed into law if considered on their own. Members often lack adequate time to study or even read the bill. The unwritten Hastert Rule dictates that the Speaker will not allow a floor vote unless most of the majority party supports it. Around the same time, perhaps fifty years ago, the usual order started breaking down. Previously, strong committees debated bills and amendments and selected the bills to go to the floor for a vote. Committee chairs were chosen by length of service, not as now by the party leadership. In the mid-90s, the Speaker began appointing all committee members. Both parties participated at various times in instituting these changes. Senior leaders decide which bills should be moved to the floor for discussion, amending, and voting. The party in power controls what happens on the floor. Today, conference committees to work out the differences between House and Senate bills are nearly extinct. If both houses are controlled by one party, its leadership meets behind closed doors and announces the outcome.

This list is just a few of the legislative abuses in Congress. Gehl and Porter say, "It is accepted as normal when the Mitch McConnell's and Nancy Pelosi's of America – currently our most powerful members of Congress – announce publicly and proudly that their top priorities are either resisting the current President or electing more members of their party."

Consequences: "The health of our democracy, long-term economic competitiveness, and shared prosperity and social progress… have been badly damaged". Lack of problem-solving is a result of dysfunction. Both parties are guilty of keeping a topic unsolved as a tool to get reelected and gain power. Our election and legislative weaknesses tend to increase the power of members with extreme views, reducing the percentage of moderates; a graph in The Politics Industry shows moderates in Congress in 1951 to have been by party 44 and 41% Vs. 11 and 6% in 2018. WOW! There is "declining bipartisan support of landmark legislation (1935-2017)". There is "No Action without a Time-Sensitive Crisis…". Trust in the federal government had dropped from 73% in 1964 to 17% in 2018.

The percentage of Independents in the U.S. has risen between 2004 and 2019 from 31% to 41%. This shows that people are unhappy with our two powerful parties. While Independents in America in 2019 stood at 41%, Democrats and Republicans respectively were at 30% and 28% per Gallup. *With both major parties now having under 31% popularity but still winning almost all seats, it is crystal clear that the flawed election machinery is to blame.* People know key changes are needed.

How to Effect Change. Gehl and Porter speak of "laboratories," meaning the states. Already some states have been experimenting with various forms of open primaries and ranked-choice voting. Our country is unusual in its states' autonomy and flexibility to try new ideas on a smaller-than-national scale.

Grassroots efforts are needed to push their state legislatures to action to make pivotal change happen.

PART V

MORE THAN TWO PARTIES

15

Takes Two to Make a Fight

One day long ago, when we were little children, my sister and I had a loud disagreement in the backyard. Our mother quickly arrived. Since I was convinced that my position was correct, meaningful, and fit my thinking about how things ought to be, I did not doubt that I would come out ahead. Instead, she showed little interest in my rationale – probably didn't even listen. She only said – as long ago as WWII, mind you – that it "takes two to make a fight." By then returning to the house, she effectively ruled this entire vitally important affair as an impasse from which neither party would gain anything.

You might ask whether our mother solved the problem or taught us a lesson. Probably not. In the metaphor of the two children being the two parties in Congress, she played the role of the voting public and took no action – even though I can testify that she had the ultimate authority over us kids.

We have only two influential parties in the Senate and House of Representatives – and generally everywhere in our country. They act like I was when I was very young. Winning is everything; it is a zero-sum game – a combative Congress. So, it does "take two to make a fight"!

Are two sides more likely to have a more severe and protracted difference of opinion than three or four? Probably so. Having more perspectives on a disagreement can soften the discussion and force the finding of common ground.

Most other countries have multiple viewpoints and positions. Their legislators know that they must get along enough to negotiate. Don't forget that we citizens are the preeminent power in America; we play the role of the "mother" in this parable and can force changes.

Let's have more ambiance – like Thanksgiving.
Negotiation and civility in Congress, not combat

16

Polarization and Dysfunction in Congress and the States Too!

Reference: The Disunited States, The Economist, September 3, 2022

The lead editorial in the referenced Economist began by focusing on the polarization we now see in state governments. The notion alludes to the founders' ideology of utilizing individual states as experimental grounds for novel concepts and measures, thereby circumventing the need for nationwide implementation. But what is happening today has degenerated into a culture war, a combative Congress. Why is this?

Of the 50 states, 37 are ruled by a single party, meaning both houses of their legislatures plus the governor's office. This makes them one-party states. Many are genuinely one-party because a preponderance of their people is conservative or liberal. Others have their elections influenced by their electoral methods. In any case, control by one party leads to less negotiation or compromise in state governments and can result in radical positions and laws. It sounds an awful lot like our federal government. This is no accident because similar electoral methods and the same passion for dominating politics and winning the "game" exist throughout the nation, because state lawmakers often rise to federal office, and last – but not least – because there are only two influential parties throughout the country making legislating a zero-sum game; each one is either winning big-time or losing big-time. There should be a career for competent problem solvers to have rewarding political careers without participating in constant battle.

The article moves from the states to the federal level and politics in general. It states that American "dysfunction" threatens the U.S.

We can have a more peaceful and collaborative Congress!

and a world that still depends on us to lead. "The federal government should stop neglecting its responsibilities... including immigration and climate change." So, what do we do about this muddy field where we find ourselves mired? The Economist article said, "...more than this, America needs electoral reform. It should end gerrymandering, which ***lets politicians choose their voters rather than vice versa***." Now there is a sentence that says it all!

Providing multi-member districts (MMD) rather than custom-designed single-member districts would lead to election results that would match the diversity of a state's population much better and eliminate the evil gerrymandering. It would increase the variety of viewpoints in legislatures. Most people don't realize that Congress in 1967 mandated by law single-member districts for the U.S. House. Ranked choice voting (RCV) also has been shown to produce fairer results and allows voters to rank their preferences for candidates in addition to their first choice. Many other countries use MMDs and RCV. RCV yields more proportional results and can eliminate runoff elections with all their undesirable issues, including cost, time, and poor voter turnout. The use of RCV should be coupled with multi-member district elections. Substituting open nonpartisan primaries for closed party primaries is needed to halt our two parties' lock on who competes in the primary and gets advanced from the primary to the general election.

The punch line of these changes in electoral methods is that they lead a country to have more than two parties. This is the objective! Over twenty leading nations have more than two influential parties. These countries have seen the advantages of getting away from two combative parties whose primary goal is to hurt the other party, not to solve their country's problems. This is not to say that strong feelings don't arise in the legislatures of these countries, but the chances of finding a negotiating partner are much improved if there is more than one from which to pick. We must have more than two viewpoints on issues and civil negotiation. See the graph in chapter 6.

Let's return to polarization. Is polarization originating in our federal and state legislatures or the populace? Well, which came first, the chicken or the egg? It doesn't matter. One feeds on the other. More civil politics would be a huge step in reducing polarization in America.

The Economist article wraps up by saying that we voters have a responsibility. Amen! We not only have a burden but also a sovereign duty. Remember what Pogo said: **"We have met the enemy, and he is us."**

17

We Must Have More Than Two Parties

Ms. Danielle Allen, a candidate for governor of Massachusetts in 2020, had an Op-Ed in the WSJ on May 7, 2022, in which she said, "We the people are healthy, but our vehicles of political participation need some attention." She said that our political parties are the only vehicle available for someone to make a case for election. ***These two parties own the mechanisms!*** She argued that many citizens have turned their backs on the parties. She said that "Our system of representation is in crisis."

Voters are more likely to take an interest if there is a candidate with whose viewpoints they agree, which becomes more probable with additional parties.

Guess what? There are known solutions. We must have more than two parties! How do we do that? We institute open primaries to replace closed-party primaries, ranked-choice voting, and multi-member districts. These all stimulate proportional voting, expanded policy viewpoints, diversity, and fertile ground for different parties. Afterward, negotiation and compromise among various perspectives will be necessary for elections, and gerrymandering and single-member districts will be the past.

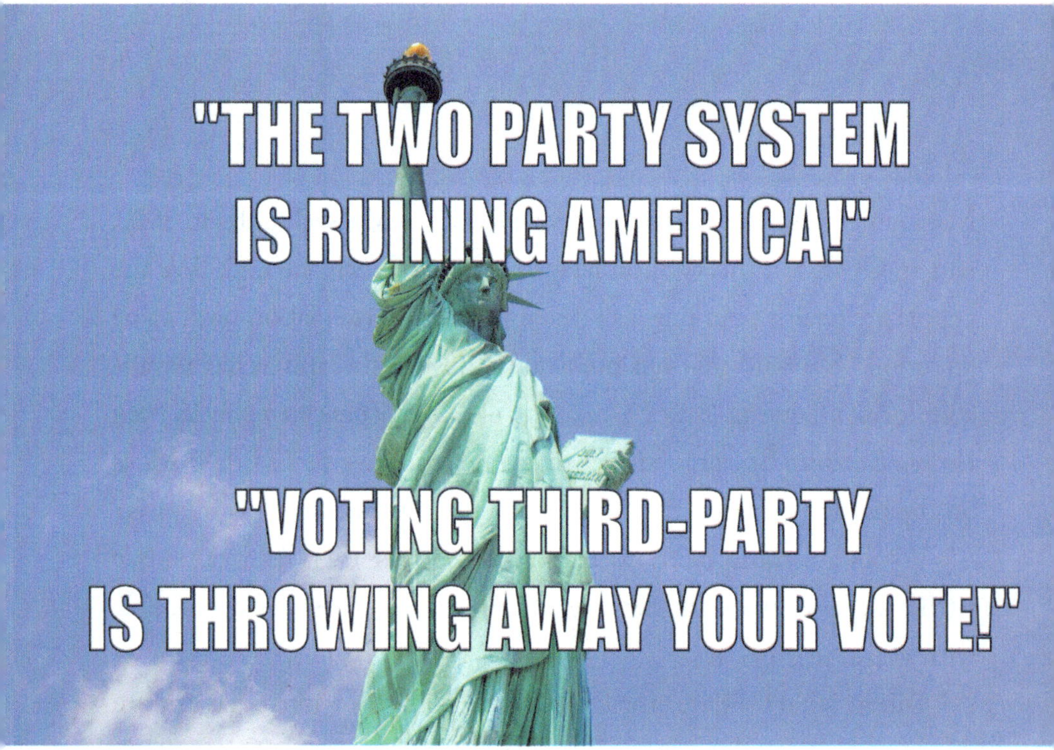

… under our current electoral methods.

It doesn't have to be that way!

18

Imagine!

Let's imagine that we have – right now – a U.S. House of Representatives populated by members from four effective parties, an effective party being defined as having at least several percent of the total number of members of the House – enough to have negotiating power on policy and votes. The number of parties rapidly increased after changes were made in electoral methods.

Now, each party has a somewhat narrower but better articulated and reasoned set of values and interests than we had experienced in the old days of only two parties. There are more viewpoints with four parties, and more voters have found members with whom they share values. We, voters, know more accurately where each member stands.

The members were elected not from single-member districts but from multi-member districts. Eliminating closed party primaries and instituting primaries open to other parties made a huge difference. These, coupled with using a proportional voting methodology called ranked-choice voting, produced elected members with a broader and better-understood range of viewpoints. It also yielded a set of members with values more proportional to those of the voting public.

Electing senators was different, but changes occurred there, also. Using proportional voting methodologies and eliminating the closed primaries to select candidates for the general election had outstanding effects. The evolution into four parties spilled over into the senate races, causing the election of senators with a greater variety of perspectives and values.

Fourth of July in a small Texas town

What changes have we noticed?

- Well, the first and most apparent were the surprises in the elections of the Speaker of the House and the Senate Majority Leader. After all, each is supposed to be the leader of everyone in the House or Senate!
- Committees operate as they did decades ago, and their chairs no longer come from one party. Other aspects of regular order and floor discussion of bills are in full bloom. Everyone is ecstatic about what happened.
- Then followed the discussion on raising the debt limit. The smaller parties carried the day by insisting on ending the past stalemates and starting with a clean sheet of paper, and they would not move on until something permanent was done.
- The immigration debate is still ongoing, but it appears that coalitions are being formed that will enact changes to immigration laws in multiple pieces of legislation rather than in a 5,280-page bill.

19

See Saw Congress

Problem

Over the past roughly 10-25 years, our U.S. Congress has evolved into a bipolar entity, this becoming increasingly obvious in the past several years.

Objective

Analyze the root causes for the dysfunction of Congress and stimulate corrections.

Analysis

There is plenty of evidence that Congress has become a constant two-party battle for control. The parties view winning and power as more important than the work for which their constituents elected them. All too often, we see validation of the axiom that the ends justify the means. Problem solving is a lost art; the big broken things remain broken – however obvious they may be.

What are the results? This polarization has brought the approval of Congress down below 20%. Respect for America has declined internally and abroad. The similar vote-getting power of the two parties has resulted in frequent "See Saws" – changes in who is in the majority – that result in massive swings in focus and reversals of what the other party just finished doing.

We have only two similar-sized parties, and the fact that they have degenerated into the present bipolar and dysfunctional mode is not unnatural. It derives from our electoral systems. Our nation's founders were very suspicious of political parties, and several of them predicted our present circumstance of having two parties constantly at war with one another. We voters are in charge in America; the monkey is on our backs to get the electoral problems fixed.

PART VI

OPEN PRIMARIES

20

Open, Nonpartisan Primaries I

Let's point out at the outset that these pages focus solely on electoral methods for the U.S. House and Senate, not any other offices.

Edward "Ned" Foley is a constitutional law professor at Ohio State University and heads its election law program. He was interviewed by Kevin Kosar of the American Enterprise Institute for an April 11, 2022, article.

Mr. Foley advocates that Congress require by law that U.S. Senators and Congresspersons be elected by majority vote – over 50%. Congress has this authority. The Constitution deals with Congress in Article I, whose Section 4, after saying that the state legislatures can regulate the holding of elections, says, "...but the Congress may at any time by Law make or alter such Regulations..."

This brought up the question of how widespread non-majority voting occurs for members of Congress. Well, the answer is grim; a lot of plurality voting is legal, meaning that the winner must have more votes than each other candidate in an election, but not a majority. This can lead to unintended consequences and is a failure in our electoral methods. Professor Foley is doing us a service by advocating changes.

Primary vote requirements by state

The map and table below detail primary election vote requirements by state.

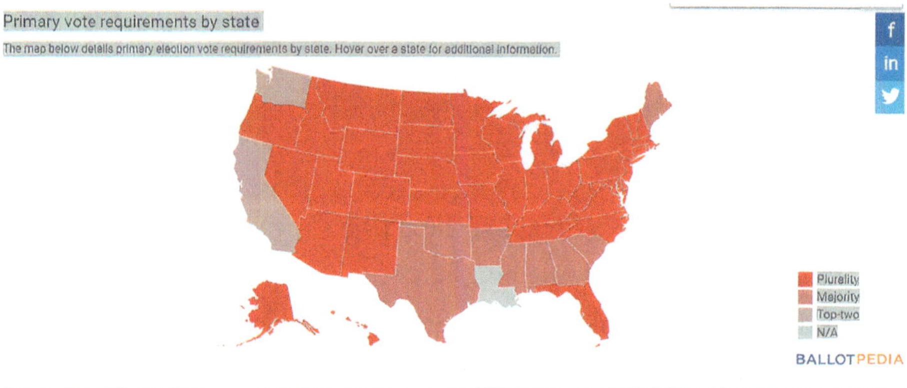

Graphic data summarized:

Plurality	39
Majority	8
Top-Two Candidates Open Primary Act(CA & WA)	2
N/A	1
TOTAL	50

During the discussion, Mr. Foley was questioned about the necessity of implementing some sort of ranked choice voting (RCV) to guarantee that the victorious candidate represents a majority. In response, he suggested employing a round-robin system, where each candidate would compete directly against every other candidate. This approach made feasible by the availability of modern-day computers commonly used for RCV, was considered a practical solution. Mr. Foley also introduced the intriguing subject of California's electoral methods, which holds significant relevance.

One can study the California system online at https://www.sos.ca.gov/elections/political-parties/no-party-preference#top-two-candidates, a detailed article by Shirley N. Weber, Ph.D., California Secretary of State.

The 2011 California law titled the "Top Two Candidates Open Primary Act" requires that all candidates for a voter-nominated office be listed on the same primary ballot. "Only the two candidates receiving the most votes – regardless of party preference – move on to the general election regardless of vote totals." One will receive a majority in the general election. Washington State has the same methodology as shown in the graphic above. Alaska now has a similar system where the top four in the primary advance to the general election, where RCV determines the winner.

The Open Primary is a huge step forward. It is the point at which two (some advocate five) candidates advance to the general election for one seat in Congress, but in contrast to the present electoral methodologies of the other 47 states, this open primary, the gateway to the general election, provides for competition among all approved parties. In 47 states, it is now virtually guaranteed that a Democrat and a Republican will be on the general election ballot, and extremely difficult for another party to have the same opportunity. This is the genesis of our two-party stalemate. Having more parties means a greater variety of viewpoints, more civility in primaries and elections, and more negotiation in Congress.

The Open Primary methodology encourages every party to be more thoughtful. Voters are more likely to vote in an Open Primary with additional choices and less influence by party leaders.

The California "Top Two Candidates Open Primary Act" provides ways a new party can get approved by the state, and they don't seem too onerous. One method requires affidavits from about 1/3 of 1% of the voters in a specific previous election. California now has five approved parties.

Comments:

- Congress can make the changes or leave it to the states. California has already tweaked The Top Two Candidates Open Primary Act to satisfy the U.S. Supreme Court.
- There are good arguments for advancing more than two candidates to an RCV general election. First, it weakens the lock our two parties now have on elections. Also, competition will tend to make political positioning more moderate.
- We can facilitate having more than two influential parties in Congress, leading to more viewpoints, civility, and partisanship.
- Both California and Washington are and have been strongly Democratic-Party states. Although new parties have been

formed, the Democrat party still dominates in both states. It will be interesting to see if voters will migrate to new parties.

- Of the 19,696,371 California voters registered for the November 6, 2018, general election: 43.5% were Democrats, 24.0% were Republicans, 5.0% were affiliated with other political parties, and 27.5% were unaffiliated ("Decline to State" or "No Party Preference") voters. It doesn't take much imagination to see that there are enough independent voters (27.5%) to make an impact, particularly if some disenchanted Democrats or Republicans join them. Voters deserve the opportunity to vote for someone other than a big-two candidate.
- What if there had been another party with, say, 5% of the Senate and the House seats these past several years – or two different parties each with 3 or 4 %? The Democrats and Republicans alike would have had to listen carefully to other viewpoints and political philosophies and soften their positions. Perhaps the small parties would refuse to vote for omnibus bills containing many unrelated issues. Implementing ranked choice voting (RCV) could have ensured that a greater number of voters' perspectives were represented and substantially diminished the incessant bickering and polarization within the nation. As a result, we might have already achieved a "functional Congress."

Root Cause Analysis:

Why do closed-party primaries lead to a combative Congress?

Due to the formidable obstacles they present, parties or candidates outside of our two prevailing political factions face a tremendously arduous task in their quest to progress to the general election and seize an opportunity to secure victory.

Why do closed-party primaries restrict the access of other parties?

Because our two parties have created laws and party rules to prevent other parties from competing?

Why is this undesirable?

Because the two dominating parties create party positions, often rigid and overshadowing those of the candidates in the primary, and because one candidate from each big party will win the party's primary, and one of these will win the general election.

The result is that a candidate from one of the two powerful parties is almost sure to win the general election. This candidate will often significantly lean to the left or right and support the party platform. The candidate will be in a combative mood and be pressured to vote consistently with the party leadership.

Closed party primaries are a root cause of our combative and dysfunctional Congress.

Actions needed:

- Re the Senate:
  - States should require a majority vote to win in a single-winner election. Senate districts are single-member districts per the Constitution, i.e., the entire state. But, instead of only having Democrat and Republican closed primaries, Senate primaries should be open, nonpartisan, and use RCV.
- Re the House:
  - Instead of only having Democrat and Republican closed primaries, primaries should use open, nonpartisan primaries using RCV. Multi-winner elections held for multi-member districts would have several winners, perhaps five, so no candidate would likely have a majority vote in either the primary or general election.

21

OPEN, NONPARTISAN PRIMARIES II

Reference: What is Final Five Voting? A Q&A with Katherine Gehl, by Kevin R. Kosar

The Congress's Electoral Methods chapter 14 discussed the significant issues with "election machinery," including the three fundamental reasons for Congress' inability to do its job well. It referenced a book by Katherine Gehl and Michael Porter referenced previously.

Ms. Gehl is also the founder of the Institute for Political Innovation and, as that name implies a careful thinker about reasons for our political dysfunctions. In September 2021, Kevin Kosar interviewed Katherine Gehl regarding our partisan primaries in America.

The primary elections in the U.S. are creations of our two powerful parties. Mostly, they have been designed to exclude competition and, in separate party primaries, pick among their party's prospects to choose a candidate to advance to the general election. This gateway or funnel virtually assures that a candidate from each party will participate in the general election and that one or the other will win. Ms. Gehl said that the problem is that we have only two choices.

Closed party primaries are the funnel, gateway, or chute to the general election.

Since voters in the present party primaries often are a relatively small portion of all voters, and since they can be the most passionate and extreme – left or right – of their party, we can and do get candidates emerging successfully from these two primaries that are not representative of the voter population. This gateway – the closed and partisan party primary is a primary (pun intended) genesis of our having only two parties more interested in winning each fracas than in solving problems of the country.

One might ask, "How is it that the rules for primaries were designed to be so restrictive?" The answer is that state legislatures made the laws governing them, and the politicians in these legislatures are almost entirely from the same two parties we have at the federal level. Many of them aspire to be in our national Congress. Recently I was at our state legislature advocating that ranked-choice voting be allowed in the state for at least a few purposes, including military voting and special elections, only to find that one of the national parties had strongly recommended that its party members vote against RCV for any purpose at the state level! Talk about a lock on electoral methods!

In the interview, Ms. Gehl discussed her advocacy for Final Five Voting, constituting two changes. First, eliminate party primaries and replace them with a single open primary allowing candidates from many parties. All registered voters can vote regardless of affiliation with any party. Second, the top five candidates advance to the general election regardless of party. There the winner is picked using instant runoff voting (ranked-choice voting), where the voter ranks the candidates, then multiple rounds of computerized voting as needed are held immediately, resulting in a winner with a majority in an election for one winner.

Open, nonpartisan primaries have the huge advantage of shifting voters' fixation toward the quality of the candidates, including integrity, education, experience, reasons for wanting the office, and personal attitudes on key important issues rather than just what party they represent. With candidates other than from the two big parties in the primary, voters will hear and respond to fresh and honest points of view, not just the party platforms. Candidates will be more civil to one another because they know those in the top five might need the second or third choice ranking in the RCV process in both the primary and the general elections.

A vital advantage of open, nonpartisan primaries is that they open the gates to additional parties. These pave the way to more ideas, better candidates who want to solve difficult problems, and a more diverse Congress where negotiation and compromise are necessary due to the chambers not being dominated by single parties. Major-party candidates will quickly learn that these open gates force a cleaning up of their acts. No longer will a single party have a lock on winning office!

This approach to solving our serious primary problem has been implemented in recent years by California, Washington, and now Alaska; California and Washington are both advancing only two candidates to the general election, which may perpetuate the two-party system. However, in just a few short years, California has experienced significant changes, including competition increases, surprise wins, and a jump in legislature approval ratings. It is still too early to see whether a change will occur in the dominance of the state by one party.

Alaska has a final-four system; it caused some dissatisfaction in 2022, but that seemed to come from candidates that lost in the RCV in the general election (not exactly a surprise) and first-time slowness in the RCV mechanics due to its novelty, Alaska's sparse population density, and perhaps inadequate preparation. The open final-four primary made much sense. These three states' actions show an increasing awareness that our tightly controlled primaries are a root cause of our issues in Congress!

PART VII

MULTI-MEMBER DISTRICTS

22

Analyzing Congress's Single-member District Mandate

Reference: Austin Plier, William & Mary Law Review, 2020

America should have more than two parties! Essentially all the world's leading democracies except the U.S. have more parties. This has been shown to provide more viewpoints, negotiation, and problem-solving. Why do we have only our two parties that have degenerated into a permanent gladiatorial relationship?

The single-member districts in the House play a crucial role in this matter. The political parties have meticulously carved out these districts, creating a confusing situation. They have deliberately drawn the boundaries so that two parties of remarkably similar sizes end up dominating most of these districts. It's mind-boggling to realize that a staggering 80-90% of these districts are deemed "safe seats," meaning that winning guarantees that a particular party advances to the general election and wins it. Consequently, the parties have become obsessed with inflicting maximum damage upon their opponents, making winning their utmost priority.

Congress voted in 1967 to mandate single-member districts in the House. Per the referenced William & Mary Law Review article, this action was triggered by a fear that states could adopt multi-member districts with winner-take-all voting to keep black candidates from winning seats. But the law since "… has had unintended and far-reaching consequences for America's national political health." "… Congress has reached peak levels of dysfunction and partisan gridlock, and the composition of Congress lags behind the growing diversity of the American electorate."

The article goes on to say that "… in the 115th Congress, every member of the U.S. House belonged to one or the other of the two major parties, leaving minor-party voters and those dissatisfied with major-party policy positions with the unenviable choice of voting their conscience – and in all likelihood, wasting their vote – or holding their noses and voting for one of the two major parties." WOW!

The article also made the case that the law was unconstitutional. Be that true or not, since Congress succeeded in requiring single-member districts, it has the power to legislate multi-member districts per Article I, Section 4 of the US Constitution. It states, "… but the Congress may at any time by Law make or alter such Regulations, except as to the Place of Choosing Senators." This action, coupled with open, nonpartisan primaries and ranked-choice voting, would provide candidates elected by more proportional voting and lead to our having more than two parties – like other democratic countries.

Root Cause Analysis

Why is Congress dysfunctional and combative?

Because our electoral methods are rigged to return candidates to Congress reliably and repeatedly. These candidates become increasingly subservient to their party, extreme, and less responsive to their constituencies.

Why is the same person elected so reliably to a seat in the U.S. House?

One of the primary factors contributing to this situation is the inherent bias in federal and state electoral laws governing Congress, which heavily favor our two main political parties. These laws create an environment where the parties have the upper hand in shaping districts to their advantage, exacerbating the problem of gerrymandering and solidifying the dominance of safe seats.

Why are these two parties able to restrict competition?

One key reason is that they were able to enact a federal law mandating single-member districts for House elections. This has been implemented by aggressive gerrymandering at the state level by both parties.

Why were these two parties able to pass this law?

As previously mentioned, the Constitution grants Congress this power, contributing to the prevalence of gerrymandered districts and partisan priorities.

Why do single-member districts facilitate the repeated reelection of one party and candidate?

Gerrymandering aims to maximize the number of reliable party-voting districts. During redistricting after each census, the controlling party manipulates boundaries to ensure their favored party's dominance in the state legislature and federal House districts.

Why can a system that many times returns a candidate to Congress be harmful?

Due to gerrymandering, minority-party voters in a district may never have a representative they voted for.

Because the single-member districts in the House, heavily gerrymandered between similar-sized parties, breed contempt for voting, leading to voter disengagement.

Because there is little or no chance for a candidate from a third party to compete successfully. This greatly diminishes the odds that fresh ideas and political philosophies will be aired in Congress.

Because a candidate who is returned repeatedly with little risk soon realizes that solving the country's problems isn't necessary to be elected. Performance isn't essential; careerism can set in.

Single-member districts are a root cause of the dysfunctionality of Congress.

23

Multi-Member Districts

You shouldn't bother to read this chapter if you love the following results that flow naturally from the present electoral systems, including single-member districts that the U.S. uses to elect its members of the House:

- Knowing that your district may never send a Representative you like to Congress.
- Having your state represented by representatives not proportional to its population's political views.
- Having only a binary choice, both of whom you dislike.
- Knowing the system is rigged, a third party with new viewpoints cannot gain any power.
- Having a government entirely dominated by two combative parties with no apparent prospect for change.
- Knowing that when the power shifts, the winning party will devote much of its energies to undoing what its opponent just finished.

Congress worked better at the time most of these Americans died for the U.S. Don't let them down.

The United States has not always had single-member districts with their gerrymandering and safe seat issues. Before 1967, the House moved back and forth between having multi-member and single-member districts. Congress enacted a law mandating single-member districts, and regrettably, it remains unchanged until today.

If we transition to multi-member districts, most states will probably end up with districts that encompass three to six seats. However, those states with smaller populations might only warrant one or two seats in the House. An election for a five-member district would select those five members. Candidates representing several parties could be on the ballot; having more parties would promote civility, negotiation, and consideration of more than two viewpoints in Congress, something badly needed in these years of polarization and perpetually kicking severe problems down the road. Elections would use a voting system like ranked choice voting to rank candidates on the ballot, facilitating fair representation, meaning those elected would represent voters more proportionally than with our present electoral systems.

Why should, or better must, America have multi-member districts for the House of Representatives?

- To encourage the existence of more than two effective political parties.
- Because having multiple effective parties promotes proportionality to the beliefs of those voting, diverse viewpoints in Congress, negotiation, and compromise in Congress, and prevents one party from having control of everything, including the House Speaker choice, committee chairpersons, rules, floor debate, etc.
- Because the present system of having a two-party dichotomy has caused constant combat in which the highest calling for both parties is damaging the other.

Advantages of Multi-member Districts

- They lead to having more than two parties and thus new viewpoints, negotiation, significantly reduced chances for autocratic control by one party, more effective committees, less overreach, and more proportional representation; primaries and elections should be facilitated by ranked-choice voting.
- Greater likelihood that voters will like one of the candidates, improving the chances of their voting.
- Much better voter satisfaction and turnout.
- Much better chance that an individual voter will have voted for someone in Congress and therefore have representation.
- Better representation of minority viewpoints.
- It puts the brakes on having only two parties whose highest calling is being against whatever the other party wants.

How can we make the needed changes?

The Constitution's Article I, Section 4 gives the states' legislatures the power to govern the election of Senators and Representatives, but goes on to say, "… but the Congress may at any time by Law make or alter such Regulations …" In 1967, Congress passed a law requiring single-member districts. It seems Congress can return power to the states to create multi-member districts or institute the requirement nationwide.

What to do?

Insist that your state legislature or Congress enacts requirements for multi-member districts!

PART VIII

RANKED CHOICE VOTING

24

Ranked Choice Voting (RCV)

Ranked Choice Voting – Defined

Ranked Choice Voting (RCV), also known as instant runoff voting, is a proportional and nonpartisan voting method. Instead of holding a separate runoff election in the future, voters can rank candidates in the order of their preference to produce an "instant runoff" result.

The graphics and descriptions below are for a single-winner RCV election, say for the U.S. House. For the general election of a multi-member district in which five house members will be elected, there might be many candidates on the ballot, and the top five would be selected using this process for a five-member district.

Voters rank candidates in order of choice. They may rank as many or as few as they please.

Votes are counted for round 1. If no one has a majority, voting goes to round 2. Before round 2, the candidate with the least number of votes is eliminated, and the second-place votes from that candidate are transferred to the remaining candidates. If this doesn't produce

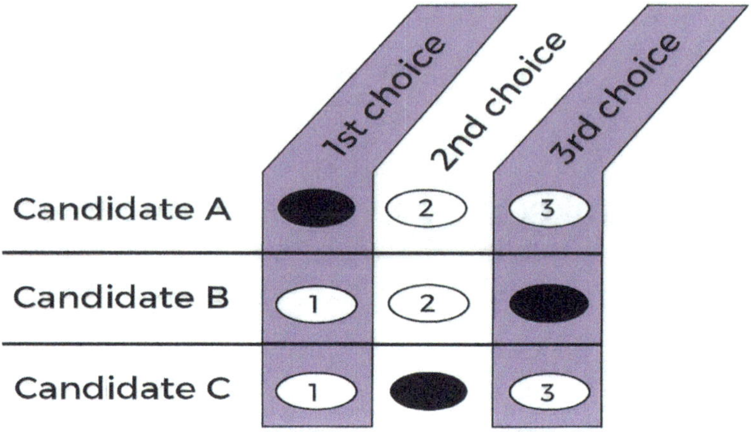

someone with a majority, the "runoff" continues with another round until there is a winner – who will have a majority.

In an election in a five-seat multi-member district using RCV, the process would produce five winners of seats using the iterative process above, but the winners would not have received a majority of the votes in the district because five winners are being elected.

Ranked Choice Voting – Advantages

RCV can replace the present "runoff" system; it is often named the *Instant Runoff* system. It produces a result during the primary or general election and eliminates the waiting time and the costs of a runoff. It also avoids the traditionally low turnout of a runoff election and, thus, the danger of selecting a winner elected by a small fraction of all voters.

RCV can replace the "first past the post" system in which the candidate with a plurality wins, i.e., there is no runoff. Now, when

How Ranked Choice Voting Works

If no candidate gets more than 50% of the vote, the count goes into an instant run off.

In this scenario, the candidate with the least amount of votes for first choice is eliminated.

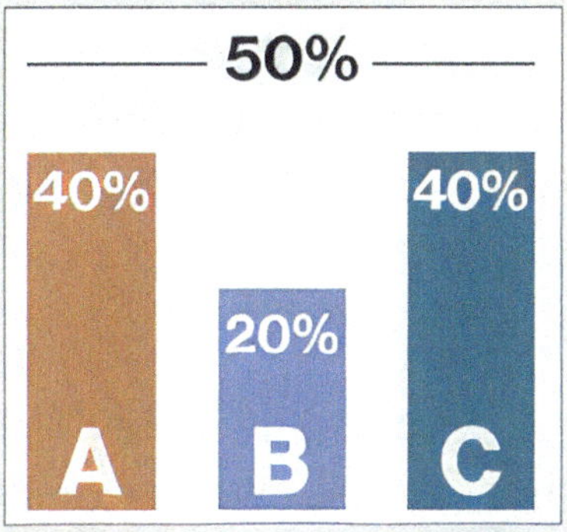

The voters who had that candidate as their first choice will then have their vote count for the candidate they marked as their second choice.

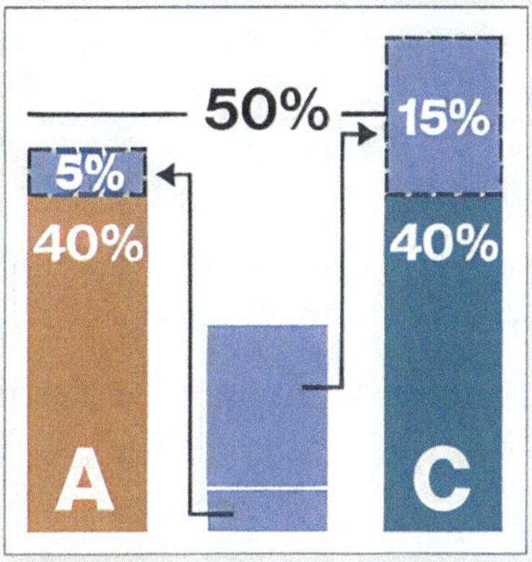

The process continues until one candidate gets more than 50% of the votes.

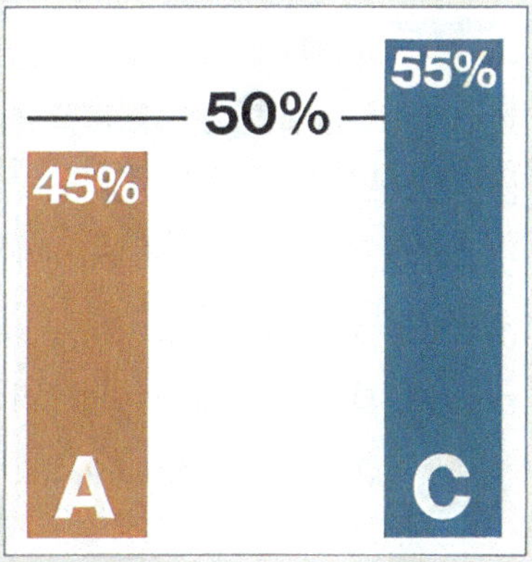

SOURCE: RANKED CHOICE VOTING RESOURCE CENTER

abc NEWS

there are more than two candidates in the race, the winner can have fewer votes than a majority and still win in many of our states with only a plurality.

Because voters can rank candidates, they aren't tempted to gamble by voting for someone they perceive is more likely to win than their favorite candidate. Ranking allows voters to rank their favorite and most likely candidates number 1 and 2 or vice versa. The spoiler effect of votes being split between candidates of similar ideologies – and wasted – is significantly reduced or eliminated.

RCV is a proportional voting system, meaning it does a much better job of electing candidates that represent the voting public fairly.

Candidates have reason to be more civil and issue-focused due to the possibility of gaining second or third-choice votes and thus having a chance to win in a later round.

Voter turnout is increased because voters feel their vote is effective. They like being able to express multiple choices by ranking, and they enjoy the increased civility of the campaigning.

RCV has been tested and is well accepted. For example, it is used in many U.S. Universities; the Academy Awards Oscars selections; internationally in Australia, New Zealand, Ireland, North Ireland, Scotland, Malta, many European countries; Maine, and now Alaska. It can be and is used in state and local elections ever more widely in the USA.

The Fair Vote website is an excellent source of additional information on RCV. Among other features, it has a very long list of entities that are using RCV.

Root Cause Analysis

Why do our primaries and general elections produce unfair results?

Because they often select candidates whom most voters do not support.

Why do they select such candidates?

Since certain primaries and elections permit winners to be decided by a plurality rather than a majority, a candidate can emerge victorious without securing over 50% of the votes.

Because others require runoff weeks or months later that is poorly attended, selecting a candidate with a fraction of the voting public.

Because voters cannot rank the candidates, this allows non-proportional outcomes in multi-candidate elections due to the spoiler effect.

Because in an election utilizing Ranked Choice Voting (RCV), candidates often adopt more moderate and courteous approaches. This is because securing second and third-preference votes can potentially lead to their victory, necessitating a broad appeal to a wider spectrum of voters.

Because RCV decreases the lock, our two parties have on winning, paving the way for additional political philosophies and parties.

Using electoral methods that select winners with plurality votes, use traditional runoffs, and avoid ranking candidates produces unfair results that the application of ranked-choice voting could eliminate. These electoral methods are root causes of the dysfunction in Congress.

PART IX

CONCLUSION

25

What do People Think is Wrong?

Knowing what our country's people think about significant issues is helpful. Statista Research conducted a study in February 2022.

It found that government and poor leadership ranked a clear #1. The other problems are almost all results of #1.

What do you think is the most important problem facing this country today?

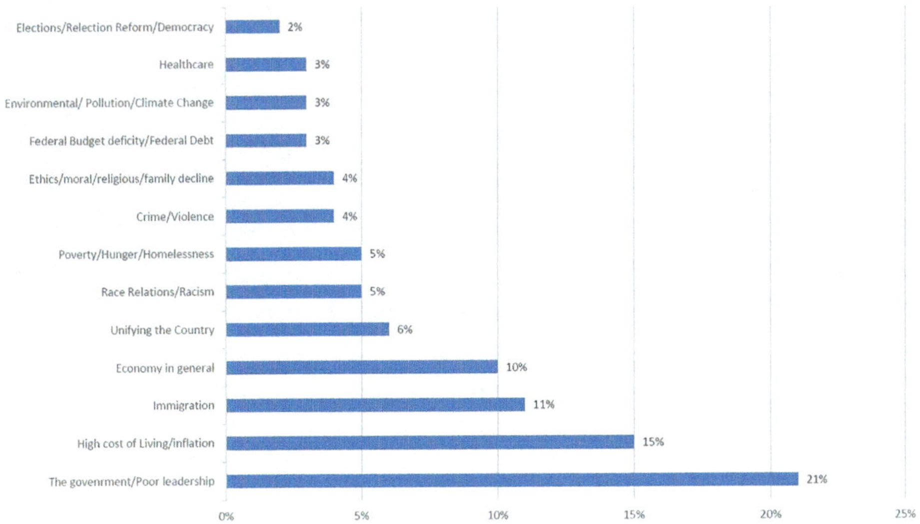

Published by "https://www.statista.com/aboutus/our-research-commitment"
Statista Research Department, Feb 22, 2023.

A couple pondering electoral methods.
Both are burdened with problems that should have been solved long ago.

26

Confidence in Congress

Gallup has measured American confidence in major U.S. Institutions annually since 1993. See their June 2022 results below.

Change in Americans' Confidence in Major U.S. Institutions, 2021-2022

Now I am going to read you a list of institutions in American society. Please tell me how much confidence you, yourself, have in each one -- a great deal, quite a lot, some or very little.

	2021 % Great deal/Quite a lot	2022 % Great deal/Quite a lot	Change pct. pts.
Small business	70	68	−2
The military	69	64	−5
The police	51	45	−6
The medical system	44	38	−6
The church or organized religion	37	31	−6
The public schools	32	28	−4
Organized labor	28	28	0
Banks	33	27	−6
Large technology companies	29	26	−3
The U.S. Supreme Court	36	25	−11
The presidency	38	23	−15
Newspapers	21	16	−5
The criminal justice system	20	14	−6
Big business	18	14	−4
Television news	16	11	−5
Congress	12	7	−5

Institutions are ranked from highest to lowest confidence in 2022.

I don't suppose the data above surprise most of you but seeing them presented this way must be very sobering. One can summarize the takeaways as follows:

- Congress is at the very bottom of the list.
- The most recent year, by any standard, is horrible, and the trend of confidence in Congress being cut almost by half in one year is worse.

Pretty obvious.

So, having evidence that we voters do not believe Congress is functioning well, what do we do?

- Continue voting the best we can with the choices the present electoral system allows us, the system having only two influential parties brought on by biased and antiquated electoral methods, and
- Tolerate the present non-proportional primary and general election systems, and
- Live with our combative two-party system that tolerates few points of view, allows almost no negotiation, has tossed out many time-tested legislative procedures, is virtually unique among important democratic nations, and is in a constant state of undeclared war.
- Or do we agree that we voters are the sovereign power in this country and want pivotal changes soon? We can do that, and Congress will enact changes if we demand them. Try the ideas below to bring about more than two parties and significant improvements!
    - Congress reverses the law that created single-member districts nationwide for the House, guaranteeing gerrymandering, safe districts, and our warring two parties. It substitutes multi-member districts. Another pathway is to do this at the state level.
    - Eliminate closed-party primaries. Substitute open primaries.

- o Institute ranked choice voting (RCV) nationwide for the House and the Senate.

These may be new concepts for many readers. If so, there are many sources on the web to learn more about them.

27

Speaker of the House Election

I decided to jot down some thoughts today, January 3, 2023, after watching on TV some of the U.S. House of Representatives voting for its Speaker position. This is one of the most powerful positions in our country, being second in line to assume the presidency, among other matters.

Of course, you know that Rep. Kevin McCarthy lost the first three ballots, and as of now, we don't know what the coming ballots will bring.

The Washington office of the Russian News Agency Tass reports, along with other news sources, that it has been 100 years since the Speaker was not elected on the first ballot. I am not pleased that power politics are so powerful in Washington that an election of this importance has been cut and dried for 100 years, so perhaps Tass was delivering good news rather than bad. We need an overhaul of Congress's elections machinery/electoral methods.

I researched the reasons the group of Republicans who opposed McCarthy gave for doing so. These reasons given were: no good-faith response for months to change the status quo; failure to demonstrate any desire to change the status quo in Washington meaningfully; refusal to consider any names suggested for committees, and refusal to commit to holding votes on policies concerning a balanced budget, the Fair Tax Act, the Texas Border Plan, and Congressional Term Limits; individual earmarks requiring a two-thirds majority to pass; and a commitment to have all amendments that would cut spending be considered on the House floor.

Requesting open and democratic consideration of important matters by voting on them is quite reasonable. The trend of the past several years for the Speaker to have almost dictatorial powers seems long overdue for reversal, and McCarthy's refusal toward openness is and should be a problem for him or any party leader.

Given this background, let's explore how having more parties might produce different results. In the present House, the Republicans have 222 of the seats, to the Democrats have 212, or 51% Vs. 49%. Our divided government always seems to have one or the other of the two warring parties with a slight majority. This is called a duopoly, a preponderant influence or control by two political powers. It isn't working well for us.

We should be strong advocates of our country having more than two influential parties, meaning parties with a high enough percentage of the elected members of Congress to influence legislation, policy, and procedures. Sometimes one hears that this means 5% or more. Why have more than two parties? Well, for starters, it is prevalent in other important countries.

When a political body has 3 or 4 influential parties, it becomes much less likely that any party has a majority and dominates. The parties must negotiate and be more civil with one another. They form coalitions to consider and pass legislation, and the coalitions will differ from one piece of legislation to the next. Parties and members must be more civil to each other because Party A might partner with Party C one week and with Party D next week. More parties will reduce the tendency of our present Congress to throw bills on many topics into one omnibus piece of legislation, thereby preventing careful consideration and transparent votes on individual issues.

Our problem with Congress is simple compared with putting a man on the moon!

Let's ponder three scenarios that might result from America making pivotal changes in its electoral systems, fostering the evolution of additional parties. Right now, the two parties have created electoral systems that ensure no other parties can evolve and prosper. What could happen in the U.S. House's Speaker election?

Scenario A - Today

Republican	51%
Democrat	49

Scenario B

Republican	45%
Democrat	44
Party X	4
Party Y	7

Scenario C

Republican	35%
Democrat	33
Party X	20
Party Y	12

We are seeing today what happens in scenario A: One side seems sure to win, even with a very slight majority. This results from block voting by the party. The winning party will provide the Speaker. The Speaker is so powerful that members of their party were afraid to contest the election for 100 years.

Let's look at scenario B. No matter how the coalitions are formed, neither the Republican nor the Democrat party has a lock on receiving a majority vote. All parties must respect the viewpoints of the others. Conceivably, even an outstanding member of party X or Y could win. The four parties almost surely would demand much fairer methods of appointing committee chairs and members. A return to regular order with competent committees and chairs is very likely. Committees decide which bills move to the floor for discussion and a vote. Making all rules of both houses of Congress would quickly become much less autocratic. The Speaker would be less powerful.

Scenario C presents an even more dramatic picture. A majority is needed to elect the Speaker, but what is essential is that the Speaker will be more to the people's liking. The Speaker could come from any of the parties. It should not be embarrassing that negotiation and several votes might be needed to choose the Speaker. After all, this is how a government is supposed to work. The four parties indeed would have different philosophies and priorities; negotiation among them to set the direction of the government will be a very positive process. The resulting legislation will be less extreme.

What is required to foster the evolution of additional parties?

- Eliminate closed-party primaries. Substitute open primaries from which a fixed number of candidates, around five, earn the right to compete in the general election.
- Used ranked choice voting where appropriate to ensure that candidates must have a majority vote to win.

- Use multi-member districts to eliminate single-member districts, a law that has made over 80-90% of the House districts safe through gerrymandering.

28

Let's Pretend

Let's pretend something that won't work your grey cells too hard. Pretend that for some years Congress's House of Representatives has had members who for the most part come from districts that have several members. Open, non-partisan primaries allow candidates from many parties. On top of that, voting methods used for both houses have endeavored to make the results proportional to those casting the votes.

We have four parties large enough to make a difference. Every two years the new members and senators elect their chamber's leaders, and it is never obvious from which parties these will come. The number one and number two leaders in each house are now often from different parties. Committee chairpersons also are from more than one party, often being the most knowledgeable and experienced person in the committee's topic. Both houses also use ranked choice voting for all these elections to ensure broad support.

It has been most gratifying to note some of the results that have ensued these past years from the electoral methods and events described above.

- U.S federal debt as a percentage of GDP is heading downward.
- Our medical system is fair to all, above average in results, and no more expensive than in most other countries.
- America is again respected by friend and foe alike.
- The Senate Foreign Relations committee, like that led by Senator William Fulbright from 1959-1974, provides valuable advice and counsel to the administration in foreign affairs.
- Members of Congress spend most of their time in Washington.

My mother used to tell me that such a tale was a flight of fantasy, but I prefer to call it a parable.

29

Pivotal Reforms Imperative for Congress

Problem

Congress has become dysfunctional due to the combat of its two parties, significantly damaging its ability to solve America's domestic and foreign problems.

What to do?

For sure, tackle the root causes rather than the symptoms.

Background

"Political parties are essential to democratic governance … America's system was designed to operate in an environment where most factions would be ephemeral, developing over issues and then dissolving when those issues faded or were somehow resolved." Adapted from The Role of Political Parties in Preventing Congress from Functioning, Dennis R. Bullock, Real Clear Policy.

We have high levels of polarization among the people in our country. One hears discussions about whether we are polarizing members of Congress or vice versa. It must work both ways, reflecting "which came first, the chicken or the egg." Reducing polarization and animosity in either camp would likely improve the other. Reforms to Congress to cause it to do its assigned tasks better would be extremely helpful to the country's mood and prosperity.

Remember that you can review the History chapter to refresh your memory of how we evolved over the past fifty-plus years to having our present combative Congress.

Results

- Two combative parties
- The very slimmest of majorities are enacting many massive laws of major consequence, a recipe for continued dissension.
- Huge pieces of legislation cover many topics as a tool to suppress dissenting points of view and pass partisan, extreme, and weakly supported ideas.
- Strong party influence in electoral methods has led to the common use of many other non-proportional electoral methods in selecting our candidates, including first-past-the-post/winner-take-all primaries and elections, runoffs that are usually very poorly attended, and the lack of ways for voters to indicate choices other than their first preference.
- Gerrymandering of the single-member districts led to around 80-90% safe seats.

- Many voters do not have anyone in Congress for whom they have voted.
- "...in the 115th Congress, every member of the U.S. House belonged to one of the two major parties, leaving minor-party voters and those dissatisfied with major-party policy positions with the unenviable choice of voting their conscience – and in all likelihood, wasting their vote – or holding their noses and voting for one of the two major parties." And "...the composition of Congress lags behind the growing diversity of the American electorate." Both comments are from a 2020 William and Mary Law Review.
- Virtually no chance of another party arising.
- Dramatic and disruptive swings in policies and legislation when power shifts from one party to the other, making it almost impossible for citizens and businesses to plan their lives.
- A decline in international respect.
- Disenfranchisement, distrust, and disgust among voters. A feeling of helplessness.

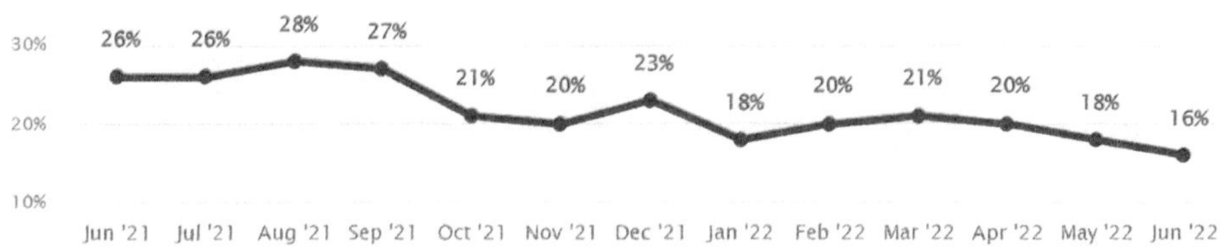

Congress Approval, Statista 2022

From

Like this car, Congress is in bad repair!

To
A beautiful Model T Ford,
portraying a reformed Congress.

Root Causes

Congress is locked into having only two effective parties. Again, see the graph in the chapter on Proportional Voting. The root causes of this deplorable situation are:

- Closed party primaries.
- Single-member districts for the House.
- Other non-proportional voting methods are used for both Representatives and Senators.

What To Do

- Eliminate closed-party primaries. Substitute open primaries from which a fixed number of winners, around five for single-winner elections and more for multi-winner elections, earn the right to compete in the general election.
- Use multi-member districts to get rid of gerrymandered single-member districts.
- Used ranked choice voting where appropriate to ensure that candidates must have a majority vote to win.

Albert Einstein said the definition of insanity is **"doing something over and over again and expecting a different result**." The point is that the solutions are at hand, and it is up to us to seize them.

We must focus on public education, hence this book. Most Americans are too accustomed to only two effective parties and to having gerrymandered single-member districts for House elections. They have not articulated the root causes of our problems nor realized that real solutions are available and within our grasp. It is disturbing that other modern democracies are now using better systems than ours; we have become accustomed to believing that America's electoral systems are the world standard. It is time to wake up and realize that our old rusty automobile needs an overhaul.

We have some staunch allies, members of Congress, who know all too well the roadblocks, overloading, inefficiencies, and severe polarization in Congress. Most feel the indignity of not being allowed to do the work their constituents hired them to do – of not having a voice of their own.

References

Drutman, Lee. *The Case for Multiparty Democracy in America*, Oxford University Press, 2020.

Eckam, Dan. *Beyond Two Parties, Why America Needs a Multiparty System and How We Can Have It*, 2019.

Gehl, Katherine M. and Porter, Michael E. *The Politics Industry, How Political Innovation Can Break Partisan Gridlock and Save Our Democracy*. Harvard Business Review Press, 2020.

White, Adam J. The Atlantic.

You Tube

www.solveamericangridlock.com

https://www.fairvote.org/

You Tube

Merriam-Webster On-line

Ballotpedia

Bullock, Dennis R. *The Role of Political Parties in Preventing Congress from Functioning*. Real Clear Policy.

Levine, Sam. *Safe Seats*. The Guardian.org. February 17, 2022.

Merriam Webster.

Wasserman, Dave. Cook Political Report, February 2022.

Proportional Representation, Ace Electoral Network.

Gallagher, Michael and Mitchell, Paul. *The Politics of Electoral Systems*. Oxford University Press. 2005.

jobenomics.com

Larimore, Rachel. *Very Expensive Week*. The Dispatch Weekly. August 27, 2023.

The Disunited States. The Economist. September 3, 2022.

Allen, Danielle. WSJ Op-Ed. May 7, 2022.

Kosar, Kevin. *Interview of Professor Ned Foley*, April 11, 2022.

Weber, Shirley N. *No Party Preference Top-Two Candidates*. www.sos.ca.gov/elections/political-parties/no-party-preference#top-two-candidates

Kosar, Kevin R. An interview of Katherine Gehl on *What is Final-Five Voting?*

Plier, Austin. *Analyzing Congress's Single-member District Mandate*. William and Mary Law Review, 2022.

Ranked Choice Voting Resource Center. Graphic.

What Do You Think is the Most Important Problem Facing the Country Today? Statista Research Department. February 2, 2023.

Change in Americans' Confidence in Major U.S. Institutions, 2021-2022. Gallup. June 2022.

About the Author

Tom Mast lives in Austin, Texas, with his wife, Eddie, of many years – many decades, in fact. They adore their two sons and five grandchildren. Tom grew up in Lubbock and Midland, Texas, received a BS degree in mechanical engineering from The University of Texas and an MS from Stanford, served as a Lieutenant in the U.S. Navy in the Philadelphia Naval Shipyard and Spain, and returned to graduate from the Harvard Business School. He spent his career in manufacturing and engineering management and has traveled widely. In recent years, he has been active in several non-profit organizations. He has long been interested in our country's polarization, the duopoly in our Congress, the causes, and what improvements we can encourage.

If you live under a rock and are not tech savvy, send him a smoke signal. However, if you are tech friendly and wish to contact him, feel free to send him an email at combativecongress@masts.us

Please Leave A Review On Amazon

Please take a few minutes to write a review for Combative Congress. It will be helpful to others, and I will greatly appreciate your making the effort.

Go to Amazon and open the page for Combative Congress, scroll down until you see on the left side the words: Review this product. The rest is easy and quick.

Made in the USA
Coppell, TX
12 December 2023

25930391R00085